John Rutter

FIVE CHILDHOOD LYRICS

for unaccompanied
mixed voices

MUSIC DEPARTMENT

OXFORD

UNIVERSITY PRESS

This work was given its first performance by the London Concord Singers conducted by Malcolm Cottle on 11 April, 1973, in the Purcell Room, London.
Duration: 9 minutes

for Malcolm Cottle and the London Concord Singers

FIVE CHILDHOOD LYRICS

JOHN RUTTER

1. MONDAY'S CHILD

Words: Traditional

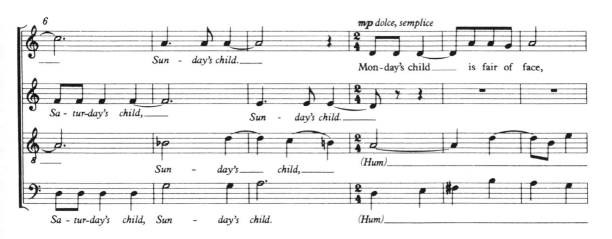

Five Childhood Lyrics

Five Childhood Lyrics

Five Childhood Lyrics

2. THE OWL AND THE PUSSY-CAT

Words by EDWARD LEAR

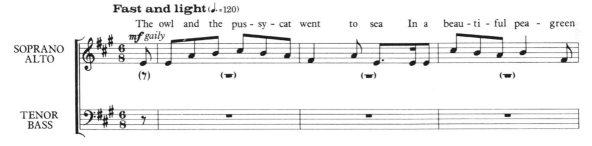

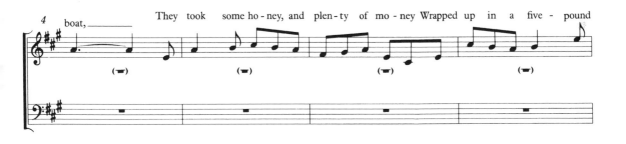

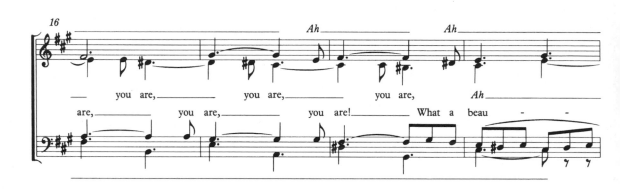

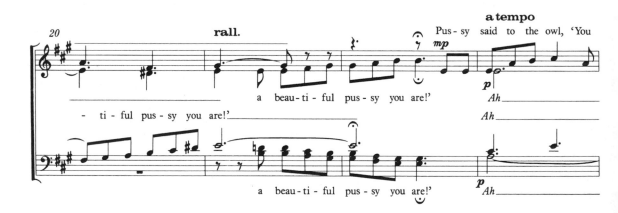

Five Childhood Lyrics

long we have tar - ried: But what shall we do for a ring?'

Ah

They sailed a - way for a

Ah

year and a day, To the land where the Bong - tree grows, And there in a wood a

pig - gy - wig stood, With a ring at the end of his

nose, his nose, his

nose, his nose, his nose, his nose, his

nose, with a ring at the end of his nose.

his nose,with a ring at the end of his nose, with a ring at the

nose, with a ring at the end of his nose, with a ring at the

nose, with a ring at the end of his nose.

Five Childhood Lyrics

a tempo

end of his nose. Ah

'Dear pig, are you wil-ling to sell for one shil-ling Your ring?' Said the pig-gy 'I

Ah

will.'_____ So they took it a-way and were mar-ried next day By the tur-key who lives on the

Ah

hill._____ They dined on mince, and sli-ces of quince, Which they ate with a run-ci-ble

lightly

spoon,_____ And hand in hand, on the edge of the sand, They

And

spoon, And hand____ in hand, on the edge of the sand,

easier alternative

Five Childhood Lyrics

Five Childhood Lyrics

3. WINDY NIGHTS

Words by R.L.STEVENSON *

*from *A Child's Garden of Verses*

Five Childhood Lyrics

Five Childhood Lyrics

Five Childhood Lyrics

Five Childhood Lyrics

Five Childhood Lyrics

16

Five Childhood Lyrics

4. MATTHEW, MARK, LUKE AND JOHN

Words: Traditional

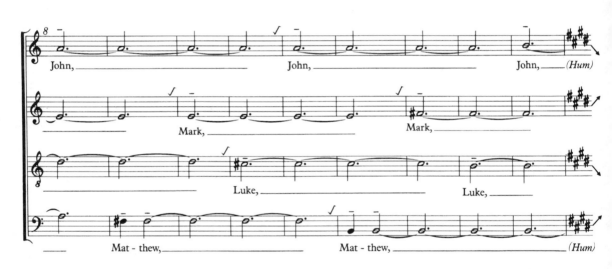

Five Childhood Lyrics

Poco più mosso (♩ = c.96)

I lie on. Four cor - ners to my

23 (Hum)

bed, Four an - gels round my

28

32 head;

S. One to watch, and one

A. And one to

T. One to watch, and one

B. And one to

5. SING A SONG OF SIXPENCE

Words and melody: Traditional

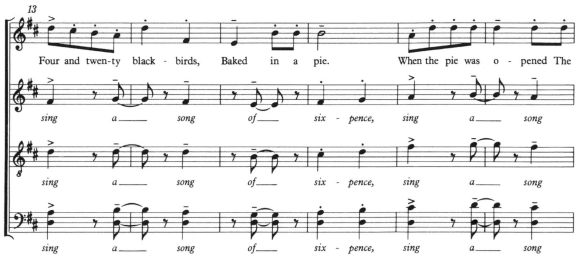

Five Childhood Lyrics

Five Childhood Lyrics

Five Childhood Lyrics

24

Five Childhood Lyrics

Five Childhood Lyrics

Five Childhood Lyrics

Five Childhood Lyrics

Reproduced and printed by
Halstan & Co. Ltd., Amersham, Bucks., England

Produced by J. P. Homer
OXFORD UNIVERSITY PRESS